ANTONIO MACHADO
Selected Poems and Prose

Translated by
Robert Bly, Will Kirkland,
Carmin Scholis and William Witherup

•

Edited by Dennis Maloney

•

White Pine Press

WHITE PINE JOURNAL

Editors: Dennis Maloney
          Steve Lewandowski

Acknowledgements
Some of these translations previously appeared in:

I Go Dreaming Roads, poems of Antonio Machado translated
by Carmen Scholis and William Witherup, Peters Gate Press,
1973 (out of print)

I Never Wanted Fame, Antonio Machado translated by
Robert Bly, Ally Press, 1979

*Publication of this journal was made possible by a grant from
the National Endowment For the Arts*

Published by
                White Pine Press
                73 Putnam Street
                Buffalo, N.Y. 14213

ISBN 0-934834-34-2

cover photo of Park Guell, Barcelona, Spain by Dennis Maloney

CONTENTS

INTRODUCTION

I

Antonio Machado is regarded by the Spanish as one of their finest poets of this century. He, along with Juan Ramon Jimenez and Miguel de Unamuno, who formed the so-called Generation of '98 ushered in a new Spanish poetics as the country entered the Twentieth Century. They, particularly Machado and Jimenez, were the fathers to a new generation of Spanish poets which included Frederico Garcia Lorca, Rafael Alberti and others.

Antonio Machado was born in Seville in 1875 and moved with his parents to Madrid in 1883. His education included seven years at the Institucion Libre de En Senanza, a liberal institute which sought to replace rote learning with an integrated approach to the development of the students' total nature. The institute instilled in the young Machado a quiet self assurance and firm moral commitment that later marked his work. In 1899 he journeyed to Paris where he worked for several months as a translator.

In 1903 he published his first volume of poems, Soledades. Four years later, he moved to the Castilian town of Soria, to take up a post as a teacher of high school French. A way, as he saw it, to make a modest living to support himself. There, in 1909, he married sixteen year old Leonor Izquiero, daughter of his landlady. Her early death in 1912 devastated Machado and he requested and received a transfer to the Andalusia town of Baeza. His deep connection and affection for her is reflected in many of the poems.

Another transfer, in 1919, brought him to Segovia and because of its proximity to the capital, Madrid, put him in touch with the intellectual life and the mainstream of events taking place in Spain. In 1931, he moved to Madrid and shortly after assumed a teaching post there with the creation of the Second Republic. Much of his writing after this date is done under the names of two apocryphal poet/philosophers he created in the persona's of Abel Martin and Juan de Mairena.

With the advent of the Spanish Civil War, Machado began a series of moves. First to Rocafort, outside Valencia, in 1936 when Madrid was threatened by Franco's troops and later with the war going bad for the Republic to Barcelona. In early 1939 he joined the exodus, helping refugees across the border into France, as the Republic fell. He died there, a month later, on February 27, 1939 in the town of Collioure.

As the title of his first book, <u>Soledades,</u> suggests, Machado was a poet of solitude. Knowing both the welcomed aloneness and the disturbing loneliness that the word implies.

His Generation of '98 had experienced the loss of the War of 1898 and with it saw the last vestiges of Spain's once huge empire disappear. This new prospect of diminished expectations turned both the nation and its poets inward to discover and celebrate the traditional villages, bare landscapes and common people of the Spanish countryside. Machado understood, well, this need to return inward and re-establish Spain's connection with itself and its people after the long period of expansion and conquest. His Spain was not in need of more political rhetoric but a few honest words as this poem translated by Bly says

> It's possible that while asleep the hand
> that sows the seeds of the stars
> started the ancient music going again.
>
> Like a note from the great harp
> and the frail wave came to our lips
> as one or two honest words.

In the spare, plain and luminous language of Machado we find both extraordinary sensitivity to place and landscapes, as well as a genuine feeling for local folklore and song as a living tradition to be learned from. His poetry is not the poetry of closed rooms but that of the open air. Many of his poems are the result of long walks through towns and hillsides. He often entered the inner world by first penetrating the outer world of landscapes and objects. Machado said "It is in the solitude of the countryside that a man ceases to live with mirrors".

Machado perfected the art of seeing. His gift was the ability to create, from the materials of the outer world transformed by his heart, a poem. An act he considered to be a collective rather than individual one. His gift of seeing was much like what the Japanese refer to as mushin or 'no mind'. It sprang from the ability to contact things directly and intimately without the imposition of the clouds of self and intellect. To look into an object or a landscape deeply without judgement.

Antonio Machado in poetry and life knew the dark side and death. Juan Ramon Jimenez described Machado as holding within himself "as much of death as of life, halves fused together by ingenuous artistry". He described his physical presence as that of an earthy hulk often clothed in baggy, dark threadbare clothes.

With the beginning of the Spanish Civil War in 1936, Machado, the poet of solitude, becomes a spokesman for the Republic, Spanish liberalism and the common man. Both under the name of his invented philosopher, Juan de Mairena and in his own prose he addressed the social, political and cultural matters at hand. Will Kirkland expands upon this period of Machado's life in his introduction to the prose section of the issue. Machado's poetry, of this period, also has the war as a backdrop in the meditations and rememberances of the once familiar landscapes of Soria and Andalusia now under control of Franco's troops and in his elegy for his fellow poet, Frederico Garcia Lorca, murdered in Granada early in the war.

III

This issue was first conceived in 1980 but was postponed due to a lack of funds. At that time, there was little of Antonio Machado's work available in translation. Only two small but fine chapbooks of translations by Robert Bly existed. Happily, in the intervening years, the situation has greatly improved. Two major collections of Machado translations by Willis Barnstone and Alan Trueblood have been published and Bly's larger selection of Machado is due out from Wesleyan Press later this year. The issue, as it now appears in your hands, contains a representative selection of Machado's poetry, arranged in roughly chronological order. The prose section includes three pieces written by Machado during the Civil War, which appear for the first time in English. These pieces, which establish Machado's ideas of the role and responsibility of the poet in the world were suppressed for decades in Franco's Spain and were found by Will Kirkland in a Cuban edition of Machado's work. They alone are worth the price of admission. We have not included the Spanish texts in order to allow for more poems with the knowledge that the several new collections out, cited above, contain the Spanish for those interested in pursuing Machado's work further.

Dennis Maloney
Editor

4

SELECTED
POEMS

I have walked along many roads,
and opened paths through brush,
I have sailed over a hundred seas
and tied up on a hundred shores,

Everywhere I've gone I've seen
excursions of sadness,
angry and melancholy
drunkards with black shadows,

and academics in offstage clothes
who watch, say nothing, and think
they know, because they do not drink wine
in the ordinary bars.

Evil men who walk around
polluting the earth . . .

And everywhere I've been I've seen
men who dance and play,
when they can, and work
the few inches of ground they have.

If they turn up somewhere,
they never ask where they are.
When they take trips, they ride
on the backs of old mules.

They don't know how to hurry,
not even on holidays.
They drink wine, if there is some,
if not, cool water.

These men are the good ones,
who love, work, walk and dream.
And on a day no different than the rest
they lie down beneath the earth.

Translated by Robert Bly

MEMORY FROM CHILDHOOD

A chilly and overcast afternoon
of winter. The students
are studying. Steady boredom
of raindrops across the windowpanes.

Recess over. In a poster
Cain is shown running
away, and Abel dead,
not far from a red spot.

The teacher, with a voice husky and hollow,
is thundering. He is an old man badly dressed,
withered and dried up,
holding a book in his hand.

And the whole child's choir
is singing its lesson:
"one thousand times one hundred is one hundred thousand,
one thousand times one thousand is one million."

A chilly and overcast afternoon
of winter. The students
are studying. Steady boredom
of raindrops across the window panes.

Translated by Robert Bly

AT A FRIEND'S BURIAL

They gave him earth one horrible afternoon
in the month of July, under the fiery sun.

One step from the open grave
there were roses with rotting petals
among sour smelling
red geraniums. The sky
pure and blue. A strong
dry breeze was blowing.

The two grave diggers
lowered the coffin,
hanging heavily from thick ropes
to the bottom of the grave . . .

And on resting it made a loud thud,
solemn in the silence.

The blow of a coffin on the earth
is something perfectly serious.

Heavy dirt clods broke
on the black box . . .

The air carried
white breath from the deep grave.

—And you, shadowless now, sleep and rest,
long peace to your bones . . .

Finally,
sleep a still and true sleep.

Translated by Carmen Scholis & William Witherup

8

I listen to the songs—
in such old meters!—
that the children sing
when they play together.
They pour out in choirs
their dreamy souls
as the stone fountains
pour out their waters:
there is eternal merriment
—a bit monotonous—
not really joyful,
and grief very ancient,
not really serious.
They pour out sad things,
sad things about love
and tales from the past.

On the children's lips
as they sing the history
is tangled but
the pain is clear;
so the clear water
tells its garbled tale
of loves long ago
that never get spoken.

Playing in the shadows
of the ancient square,
the children go on singing . . .

The stone fountain
was pouring out its eternal
river of story.

The children were singing
their innocent songs,
of something which is in motion
yet never arrives:
the history is tangled
but the pain is clear.

The tranquil fountain
continues telling its things;
the history gone,
the pain has found words.

The square and the brilliant orange trees
with their fruit round and joyful.

Uproar of the young students
piling in confusion out of the school —
they fill the air of the shady square
with the gladness of their fresh voices.

Childlike gaiety in the nooks
of dead cities!
And something we once were, that we still
see walking through these old streets!

APRIL BLOSSOMED

April blossomed
before my window.
I saw two sisters
among the jasmine
and the white roses
of a flowered balcony.
The younger was sewing;
the older spinning . . .
Among the jasmine
and the white roses
the smallest,
rosy and smiling —
her needle in the air —
looked toward my window.

The older kept turning,
silent and pale,
the spindle on its staff,
winding the flax.
April blossomed
before my window.

One clear afternoon
the older was crying
among the jasmine
and the white roses
and in front of the white flax
she threaded on the distaff.

"What's wrong", I said,
"pale silent girl?"
She pointed to the dress
that her sisten began.
The needle shone
in the black tunic;
the silver thimble
on the white veil.
She pointed out
the sleeping April afternoon,

while the bells were heard ringing.
And in the clear afternoon
she showed me her tears . . .
April blossomed
before my window.

It was another bright April
and another lazy afternoon.
The flowered balcony
was deserted . . .
Not the little one
smiling and rosy,
nor the sad sister,
silent and pale,
not the black tunic
nor the white veil . . .
The flax was turning
by an invisible hand,
all alone on the spindle,
and in the dark room
the moon of the clean
mirror shone . . .
Among the jasmine
and the white roses
of the flowered balcony
I looked at myself
in the clear moon of the mirror
which dreamed far away.
April blossomed
before my window.

Translated by Carmen Scholis
and William Witherup

Close to the road we sit down one day.
Now our life amounts to time, and our sole concern
the attitudes of despair which we adopt
while we wait. But She will not fail to meet us.

Translated by Robert Bly

YESTERDAY MY SORROWS WERE

Yesterday my sorrows were
like silkworms
that were working cocoons;
today they are black butterflies.

From how many bitter flowers
have I removed white wax!
Oh time when my troubles
worked like bees!

Today they are like wild oats,
or rye at sowing time,
like wheat smut grown into ears,
like worms in wood.

Oh time when my sorrows
had good tears,
and were like well water
that irrigates a garden!
Today they are torrential rains
that snatch mud from the earth.

Sorrows that yesterday made
my heart a hive
treat my heart today
like an old wall:
they want to tear it down, and quickly,
with a pickax blow.

*Translated by Carmen Scholis
and William Witherup*

THE WATER WHEEL

The afternoon arrived
mournful and dusty.

The water was composing
its contrified poem
in the buckets
of the lazy water wheel.

The mule was dreaming—
old and sad mule!
in time to the darkness
that was talking in the water.

The afternoon arrived
mournful and dusty.

I don't know which noble
and religious poet
joined the anguish
of the endless wheel

to the cheerful music
of the dreaming water,
and bandaged your eyes—
old and sad mule! . . .

But it must have been a noble
and religious poet,
a heart made mature
by darkness and art.

Translated by Robert Bly

Last night, as I was sleeping,
I dreamt—marvellous error!—
that a spring was breaking
out in my heart.
I said: Along which secret aqueduct,
Oh water, are you coming to me,
water of a new life
that I have never drunk from?

Last night, as I was sleeping,
I dreamt—marvellous error!—
that I had a beehive
here inside my heart.
And the golden bees
were making white combs
and sweet honey
from my old failures.

Last night, as I was sleeping,
I dreamt—marvellous error!—
that a fiery sun was giving
light inside my heart.
It was fiery because I felt
warmth as from a hearth,
and sun because it gave light
and brought tears to my eyes.

Last night, as I slept,
I dreamt—marvellous error!—
that it was God I had
here inside my heart.

Translated by Robert Bly

Is my soul asleep?
Have those beehives that labor
at night stopped? And the water—
wheel of thought,
is it dry, the cups empty,
wheeling, carrying only shadows?

No my soul is not asleep.
It is awake, wide awake.
It neither sleeps nor dreams, but watches,
its clear eyes open,
far off things, and listens
at the shores of the great silence.

Translated by Robert Bly

Clouds ripped open; a rainbow
gleaming already in the sky,
the fields entirely folded inside
the glass bell of rain and sunlight.

I woke up. What had clouded
the magical windowpanes of my dream?
My heart beat
astonished and upset.

The flowering lemon tree,
the cypress in rows in the garden,
the green field, the sun, the water, the rainbow!
drops of water in your hair. . .!

And it all vanished back inside
like a soap bubble in the wind.

Translated by Robert Bly

And he was the demon of my dreams, the most handsome
of all angels. His victorious eyes
blazed like steel,
and the flames that fell
from his torch like tears
lit up the deep dungeon of the soul.

—Will you go with me? No, never! Tombs
and dead bodies frighten me.
But the hand of iron
took mine.

—You will go with me . . . and in my dream I walked
blinded by his red torch.
And in the dungeon I heard the sound of chains
and the stirrings of beasts that were in cages.

Translated by Robert Bly

From the doorsill of a dream they called my name . . .
It was the good voice, the voice I loved so much.

—Listen: will you go with me to visit the soul? . . .
A soft stroke reached up to my heart.

—With you always . . . And in my dream I walked
down a long and solitary corridor,
aware of the touching of the pure robe,
and the soft beating of blood in the hand that loved me.

Translated by Robert Bly

If I were a poet
of love, I would make
a poem for your eyes as clear
as the transparent water in the marble pool.

And in my water poem
this is what I would say:

"I know your eyes do not answer mine,
they look and do not question when they look:
your clear eyes, your eyes have
the calm and good light,
the good light of the blossoming world, that I saw
one day from the arms of my mother."

Translated by Robert Bly

It doesn't matter now if the golden wine
floats abundantly in your crystal glass,
or if the bitter juice clouds the pure glass . . .

You know the secret passageways
of the soul, the roads that dreams take,
and the calm evening
where they go to die . . . There the good and silent spirits

of life are waiting for you,
and one day they will carry you
to a garden of eternal spring.

Translated by Robert Bly

The wind, one brilliant day, called
to my soul with an aroma of jasmine.

"In return for this jasmine odor,
I'd like all the odor of your roses."

"I have no roses; I have no flowers left now
in my garden . . . All of them are dead."

"Then I'll take the waters of the fountains,
and the yellow leaves and the dried-up petals."

Then the wind left . . . I wept. I said to my heart,
"What have you done with the garden given to you?"

Translated by Robert Bly

The house that I loved so much
—she lived there—
rising above a great mound of bricks and chunks,
    broken down
and collapsed,   shows now
its black and worm-eaten
badly-lasting skeleton of wood.

The moon is pouring down
her clear light in dreams that turn
the windows silver. Poorly dressed and sad,
I go walking along the old street.

Translated by Robert Bly

Like Anacreonte,
I want to sing, and to laugh, and to throw
to the wind
the sophisticated sarcasms, and the sobering proverbs.

And I want even more to get drunk—
you know about it—bizarre!
A true faith in dying, a thin joy,
and a funeral dance for passing time.

Translated by Robert Bly

Oh evening full of light!
The air hovers enchanted.
The white stork
sleeps as he flies,
and the swallows cross and recross, the pointed wings
stretched out in the golden wind,
in the glad evening wheel far off
flying, dreaming . . .

And one turns back like an arrow,
his pointed wings stretched out in the darkening wind,
finding his black hole in the rooftiles!

And the white stork,
shaped like a hearth-hook,
serene and deformed—so absurd!—
on the belltower!

Translated by Robert Bly

FIELD

The afternoon is dying
like a simple household fire that goes out.

There, above the mountains,
a few coals are left.

And that tree on the white road, broken,
makes you cry with compassion.

Two branches on the torn trunk, and one
leaf, withered and black, on each branch!

Are you crying now? . . . In the golden poplars
far off, the shadow of love is waiting for you.

Translated by Robert Bly

It's possible that while asleep the hand
that sows the seeds of stars
started the ancient music going again

Like a note from the great harp —
and the frail wave came to our lips
as one or two honest words.

Translated by Robert Bly

REBIRTH

Corridors of the soul! The soul that is like a young woman!
You clear light
and the brief history
and the joy of a new life . . .

Oh turn and be born again, and walk the road,
and find once more the lost path!

And turn and feel in our own hand
the warmth of the good hand
of our mother . . . And walk through life in dreams
out of love of the hand that leads us.

* * * *

In our soul everything
moves guided by a mysterious hand:
ununderstandable, not speaking,
we know nothing of our own souls.

The deepest words
of the wise men teach us
the same as the whistle of the wind when it blows,
or the sound of the water when it is flowing.

Translated by Robert Bly

You can know yourself, if you bring up
those muddy scenes from your past dreams,
today, this sad day, when you walk
awake, open-eyed.

Memory is good for one astonishing
thing it does: it brings dreams back.

Translated by Robert Bly

TO A DRY ELM

From the old elm, split by lightning
and rotting the the center,
a few green leaves have sprouted
because of the April rain and May sun.

The hundred year old elm on the hill
licked by the Duero! A yellowish moss
stains the bleached bark
of the worm-eaten and crumbling trunk.

It won't be, like the singing poplars
that guard the road and the banks,
a home to brown nightingales.

An army of ants in a column
climbs over it, and spiders weave
their gray cloth in its insides.

Before you are destroyed, elm by the Duero,
by the woodcutter's axe, and the carpenter
changes you into a bell clapper,
a wagon pole or cart yoke;
before you burn red on the hearth tomorrow
for some poor little house
by the side of the road;
before a whirlwind uproots you
and the blast from the white sierras cracks you;
before the river pushes you into the sea
through valleys and gorges,
elm, I want to write in my notebook
the gracefulness of your green branch.
My heart waits
also, leaning toward light and life,
for another miracle of spring.

*Translated by Carmen Scholis
and William Witherup*

"THERE IN THAT MOUNTAINOUS LAND"

   There, in that mountainous land,
where the Duero River draws back
its cross-bow
around Soria, among lead-colored hills,
and patches of worn-out oaks,
my heart is walking about, daydreaming . . .

   Leonor, do you see the river poplars
with their still branches?
You can see Moncayo, bluish and white: give me
your hand, and we will walk.
Through these fields of my country,
with their embroidery of dusty olives,
I go walking alone,
sad, tired, thoughtful and old.

Translated by Robert Bly

"ONE SUMMER NIGHT"

   One summer night—
my balcony door stood open
and the front door also—
death entered my house.
He approached her bed—
not even noticing me—
and with very fine hands
broke something delicate.
Death crossed the room, not
looking at me, in silence,
a second time. What did you do?
He did not answer.
I saw no change in her,
but my heart felt heavy.
I know what broke—
A thread between us!

Translated by Robert Bly

THIRTEEN POEMS CHOSEN
FROM MORAL PROVERBS AND FOLKSONGS

I

I never wanted fame,
nor wanted to leave my poems
behind in the memory of men.
I love the subtle worlds,
delicate, almost without weight,
like soap bubbles.
I enjoy seeing them take the color
of sunlight and scarlet, float
in the blue sky, then
suddenly quiver and break.

II

Why should we call
these accidental furrows roads?
Everyone who moves on walks
like Jesus, on the sea.

III

Let us sing together: know? We know nothing.
We come from a hidden ocean, and go to an unknown ocean.
And between those two mysteries there is a third serious puzzle;
one key we know nothing of locks three chests.
The light illuminates nothing, and the wise man teaches nothing.
What does human language say? What does the water in the
    rock say?

IV

Oh, I daydreamed as a boy
about the heroes of the Iliad!
Ajax was stronger than Diomedes,
Hector stronger than Ajax,
and Achilles strongest of all; because
he was the strongest! . . . Innocent ideas of boyhood!
Yes, I daydreamed as a boy
about the heroes of the Iliad!

V

Put out on the fields
a physical laborer, a thinker, and a poet.
You will see how the poet is enthusiastic
and silent, the thinker looks and thinks . . .
The laborer looks around, probably,
for blackberries and mushrooms.
Take them to the theatre,
and only the laborer isn't bored.
The one who prefers what is alive
      over what is made-up
is the person who writes, dreams, or sings.
The head of the physical laborer
is full of fantasies.

VI

I love Jesus, who said to us:
Heaven and earth will pass away.
When heaven and earth have passed away,
my word will remain.
What was your word, Jesus?
Love? Affection? Forgiveness?
All your words were
one word: Wakeup.

VII

    There are two sorts of consciousness:
one involves light, one patience.
One involves bringing a little luminosity
to the dark ocean;
the other has more guilt—
with a net or pole, one waits
like a fisherman, for fish.
Tell me: Which is best?
Religious consciousness
that sees in the deep ocean
fish alive,
going their way,
that will never be caught.
Or this job I have, boring,
picking fish from the net
and throwing them on the sand, dead?

VIII

    It is good knowing that glasses
are to drink from,
the bad thing is not to know
what thirst is for.

IX

    You say nothing is created new?
Don't worry about it, with the mud
of the earth, make a cup
from which your brother can drink.

X

You say nothing is created new?
Potter, go to your shed.
Make your cup, and don't worry
if you aren't able to make clay.

XI

All things die and all things live forever;
but our task is to die,
to die making roads,
roads over the sea.

XII

To die . . . To fall like a drop
of water into the big ocean?
Or to be what I've never been:
a man without a shadow, without a dream,
a man all alone walking,
without a mirror, and with no road?

XIII

Mankind owns four things
that are no good at sea:
rudder, anchor, oars,
and the fear of going down.

Translated by Robert Bly

TO JUAN RAMON JIMENEZ

for his book Arias tristes

It was a May night,
blue and quiet.
The full moon shone
above the cypress,

lighting up the fountain
where the spouting water
sobbed intermittently.
Only the fountain in the silence.

Later the accent
of a dark nightingale.
A gust of wind broke
the fountain's arc.

And a sweet melody
wandered over the whole garden;
a musician played his violin
among the myrtles.

It was a sad tune
of youth and love
for the moon and the wind,
the water and the nightingale.

"The garden has a fountain
and the fountain a chimera . . ."
Sang an aching voice,
soul of the springtime.

Voice and violin grew silent,
muffling their melody.
The melancholy remained
wandering over the garden.
Only the fountain in the silence.

*Translated by Carmen Scholis
and William Witherup*

29

ABEL MARTIN'S LAST LAMENTATIONS

Today it was spring;
I dreamt that a slender body followed me
like an obedient shadow. It was
my boyish body, the one who took
the stairs three at a time.
   "Hello there, old runner!" (The deep mirror
altered the acquarium light
to a harsh light over the bone yard.)
   "Are you with me, speedy?"
                              "With you, old man."

Then I seemed to see the rows
of cypress and lemon trees in the garden,
chill cobblestones with warm pigeons,
and the red kite high in the blue sky,
and some stern angel who watched
over the magic anguish of childhood.
   Everything distant and disappeared
came back, as I dreamed, as fresh as dawn;
in the bow drawn back, firm, the arrow
of tomorrow, the terrifying sight
of the flame that has caught in the fuse
near its charge . . .
                    Oh Time, what is here now,
full of what can still happen,
you are with me on the cold path, you weave
together our hope and our reluctance to wait!

Translated by Robert Bly

DEATH OF ABEL MARTIN

> Thinking that he wasn't seeing
> because God wasn't looking at him,
> Abel said when he was dying:
> What was given has ended.
>
> Juan de Mairena: Epigrams

I

The last swifts are circling
the bell tower;
children are shouting, jumping, fighting.
In his corner the recluse, Martin.
Evening, almost night, dusty,
the childhood noise and uproar
the same, from twelve to fifty!

Oh full soul and empty spirit,
before the smoky fire,
with flame crackling from roots,
frontier fire
lighting up the deep scars!

He who lives is lost, Abel would say.
Oh, distance, distance!, that the star
no one touches, guides.
Whoever sailed without it?
Distance for the eye—oh remote ship!—
absence to the hardened heart
and soothing balm
with love's honey, holy forgetfulness.
Oh great knowledge of zero, of savory
ripe fruit that only man tastes,
water of sleep, dark source,
divine shadow of the majestic hand!
Before Day comes to me, if it comes,
the uncreated light which sees,
drown this evil howling,
Lord, with the essence of your Nothingness.

II

The angel who knew
his secret blocked Martin's way.
Martin gave him what money he had.
Pity? Maybe. Fear of the spell? Perhaps.
Martin knew solitude
that cold night; he thought
that God did not see him,
and he walked in his mute desert.

III

And he saw the aloof muse,
standing next to his bed, dressed in mourning,
the lady of his streets, fugitive,
impossible to love and always loved.
Abel said to her: "Lady,
eager to see your uncovered face
I have practically lived near daybreak
until feeling my blood grow stiff.
Today I know that you are not who I thought;
but I want to look at you and thank you
for how often you kept me company
with your cold scorn."
                    Death wanted
to smile at Martin, but didn't know how.

IV

I lived, I slept, I dreamed and have even created—
Martin thought, his pupil already cloudy—
a man who watches over
the dream, something better than what is dreamed.
But if an equal fate
waits for the dreamer and the guardian,
for him who drew roads
and for him who followed roads, panting,
creation, in the end, is only your sheer nothingness,
your giant shadow,
the divine blindness of your gaze.

V

    And anguish was followed by fatigue,
which feels his desperate hope,
the thirst that is unrelieved by pure water,
the bitterness of poisoned time.
This lyre of death!
                  Abel touched
his wasted body.
Wasn't He who sees everything looking at him?
And this slowness, blood of forgetfulness.
Oh, save me, Lord!
                 His whole life,
his incurable history appeared,
written in soft wax.
And must the new day's sun erase you?
Abel stretched his hand out
toward the vermillion light
of a warmer summer dawn, which had
already reached the balcony of his old house.
Blind, he asked for light he could not see.
Later he peacefully lifted
to his cold mouth the clean glass
of pure shadow—oh pure shadow!—full.

*Translated by Carmen Scholis
and William Witherup*

SONG TO GUIOMAR

Your poet
thinks of you. The distance
is lemon and violet,
the countryside still green.
You come with me, Guiomar.
The day goes from oak grove
to oak grove, wearing itself out.
The train devours and devours
day and rail. The Spanish broom
turns to shadow; the gold
from the Guadarrama washes away.
Because a beautiful woman and her lover
are running away, breathless,
the full moon follows them.
The hidden train resonates
inside a huge mountain.
Barren fields, high sky.
Across granite mountains
and others of basalt,
is the sea and infinity at last.
We are going together; we are free.
Although God, as in the story
a proud king, may ride bareback
on the wind's best charger,
although he may swear to us, violently,
his vengeance,
although he may saddle thought,
free love, no one reaches it.

Today I write to you in my traveler's cell
at the hour of an imaginary rendezvous.
The heavy rain breaks the rainbow in the air,
and on the mountain its planetary sadness.
Sun and bells in the old tower.
Oh evening living and quiet
which places nothing moves next to everything moves,
childlike evening that your poet loved!
And adolescent day—
light eyes and dark muscles—
when you thought of Love, beside the fountain,

kissing your lips and holding your breasts!
Everything in this April light becomes transparent;
everything in the today of yesterday, the Yet
of which in its late hours,
time sings and tells,
is based on a single melody,
which is a chorus of evenings and dawns.
For you, Guiomar, this nostalgia of mine.

*Translated by Carmen Scholis
and William Witherup*

COPLAS

When the heavens thunder
(How fine it is
for blasphemy!)
and there is smoke upon the sea . . .

The blasts of February
lash the lemon trees.
I do not sleep so I will not dream.

Translated by Will Kirkland

THE CRIME WAS IN GRANADA

I The Crime

He was seen, walking through the guns
down a long street,
coming out to the cold fields
still covered with stars, in the dark before dawn.
They murdered Federico
when the first light appeared.
The squad of executioners
dared not look him in the face.
They all closed their eyes;
they prayed: not even God can save you!
Federico fell, dead
—blood on his forehead   and filled full of lead—
. . . it was there, in Granada, you must understand
the crime was there—poor Granada!—in his own Granada . . .

II The Poet and Death

He was seen walking alone with Her,
unafraid of her sickle.
By now the sun from tower to tower; the hammers
on anvils on anvils, on anvils in forges.
Federico was talking.
He was flattering Death. She was listening.
Because yesterday in my verses, my friend,
the slap of your dry palms sounded
and you gave ice to my song, and the edge
of your silver scythe to my tragedy,
I will sing you the flesh you no longer have,
the eyes are missing,
your hair the wind shimmered,
your lips of red where they kissed you . . .
How good to be alone with you
my gypsy, Death, today as yesterday
in these breezes of Granada, my own Granada!"

III

He was seen walking . . .
          Now, build a mound,
my friends, to bury the poet,
of stone and dreams, in the Alhambra,
over the fountain where the water may weep
and say eternally
the crime was in Granada, in his own Granada!

> This was Machado's first poem
> about the war. It was written
> about two months after Lorca's
> murder.
>
> *Translated by Will Kirkland*

Madrid! Madrid! How good to say your name!
A mighty seawall for the many Spains!
The heavens thunder, the earth is torn to shreds,
you are smiling, your belly filled with lead.

> Written in 1937 while fleeing
> to Valencia from the fascist
> attack on Madrid.
>
> *Translated by Will Kirkland*

TODAY'S MEDITATION

The fiery palm tree in front of me,
just now abandoning the setting sun,
in the late and silent afternoon,
inside this peaceful garden,
while flowery old Valencia
drinks the Guadalaviar waters—
Valencia of delicate towers,
in the joyful sky of Ausias March,
her river turns entirely into roses
before it arrives at the sea—
I think of the war. The war
is like a tornado moving
through the bleak foothills of the Duero,
through the plains of standing wheat,
from the farmlands of Extremadura
to these gardens with private lemons,
from the grey skies of the north
to these salty marshes full of light.
I think of Spain, all of it sold out,
river by river, mountain by mountain, sea to sea.

Translated by Robert Bly

EVERYTHING BETRAYED

A hateful hand has drawn, my Spain
—great lyre set towards the sea, between two seas—
war zones, military plumes, on these—
plains and ridges, hills and mountain range.

The wandering dead, in hate and cowardice,
cut the wood from your oak groves,
grind the corn your soil grows,
trample golden berries in your press,

Once more—one more!—unhappy Spain!
whatever drowns in sea and wind,
treason's toy swims on, whatever truth
God's temple holds, forgetting stains,
whatever's purified by breast of earth
is offered to ambition, everything betrayed!

Translated by Will Kirkland

SONG

The moon is rising now
over the orange grove.
Venus shines like a little crystal bird.

The sky is amber and beryl
behind the distant mountains,
and the quiet sea
like mulberry porcelain.

Now it is night in the garden —
the water in its pipes —
and it smells only of jasmine,
the nightingale of scents.

How the war seems
to sleep from sea to sea,
while flowering Valencia
drinks the Guadalaviar!

Valencia of delicate towers
and soft nights, Valencia,
will I be with you
when I can't see you,
where sand spreads in the fields
and the violet sea grows distant?

*Translated by Carmen Scholis
and William Witherup*

40

TO LISTER, COMMANDER OF THE ARMIES OF THE EBRO

Your letter—oh noble watchful heart,
Spaniard indomitable, powerful fist—
your letter, heroic Lister, comforts
this that weighs on me, the deathly flesh.

In your letter I have heard the clamor
of the sacred struggle over Iberian ground:
by smells of rosemary and powder
my heart too, has been aroused.

Where the conch shell proclaims
the Ebro arrives, and from the cold steeps
where the signature of Spain begins,

from mountain to sea, these words from me:
If my pen were worth your pistol, Captain,
I would die, happily.

Translated by Will Kirkland

41

THE VOICE OF SPAIN

To the intellectuals
of Soviet Russia

Oh Russia, noble Tussia, holy Russia,
one hundred times over, noble and holy
since you gripped the hammer and sickle
when the staff and sceptre broke!,
on this occidental promontory,
over these high lands
bristling with mountains, vast lyres
of sun and stone, over its wheat colored plains
and over green fields,
its rivers deep, its clear watered shores,
beneath the black oak and the gold lemon grove,
alongside carnations and the budding broom,
from mountain to mountain and river to river
can you hear the voice of Spain?
While the war thunders
from sea to sea, she cries to you: My Sister!

October 1937, unpublished
during Machado's lifetime.

Translated by Will Kirkland

SELECTED PROSE

Will Kirkland

ANTONIO MACHADO AND THE CIVIL WAR

It has been said that the sacrifice of two poets, Frederico Garcia Lorca and Antonia Machado, opened and closed the Spanish Civil War. Garcia Lorca, 38 years old, was murdered by a fascist firing squad in Granada, August 19, 1936, one month after the guns sounded in Madrid announcing the fascist rising against the Republic. Machado, 64 years old and in failing health died just across the Catalan border, in France, February 22, 1936 four days before the fascists took Barcelona and claimed final victory over Spain.

Interestingly, their fates as poets and as men, in the U.S., serve more as sad mirrors of the de-politicizing prejudices of the culture industry than as accurate reflections of their actual lives which were involved in the political as well as the poetical currents of the times.

On the one hand Garcia Lorca, without doubt one of the great poets of this century, has been so canonized, has reached such heights of fame, that it is thought by many that no one else comes close to his poetic gifts. This canonization is not one based on the evidences of his poetry alone or even of an exemplary life; it rises out of a long process of mytholization that began at the moment of his death: he became the perfect symbol, the evidence incarnate of fascist brutality against culture and humanity: Federico was fallen innocence. As part of that claim it is advanced that he had no interest in politics. It isn't true. Though neither could anyone claim the opposite for him; he held no identifiably ideological "leftist" views. But American culture demands the simplification of all, the production of saleable Saints and Super-Heroes, little served by inquiries into full flesh and boned existences—which in Lorca's case included the delivery of the welcoming speech to Rafael Alberti on his return from Russia in February, 1936, and the reading of an anti-fascist manifesto.

His position as a de-politicized Super Poet is a useful one. It helps keep in obscure shadows the poetic and human stature of others, say of Rafael Alberti, a communist for years, who for

Machado, was the other leading young poet alongside, or even above, Lorca in the years before the war and who continues to write, to exhort and inspire today. It is convenient that Alberti need not be poetically acknowledged here since his politics are his politics are so distasteful.

And there is Machado himself, a poet of equal, and many would say, of greater rank than Lorca, yet he has only recently come to be known in the U.S., completely overshadowed by his martyred friend. Machado's death was not so spectacular, nor so opportune for martyr makers: an old man, running, with mother and brother, loyal to his defeated government, he died, as it was said of Pablo Neruda, 35 years later, of a broken heart.

Finally, among the cogniscenti he is beginning to take his place. But sadly, many want him to take it stripped of his own life, to have him live in that strangely lit poetic world, eccentrically colored, where a poet is a poet is a poet, nothing more; a man who never thinks about the price of bread or why the price is so, nor of the wars and rage around him. Yet Machado was not, no more than was Garcia Lorca, a man like that: men like that are made to special order, they do not live.

Machado declared himself immediately and openly on the side of the Republic, a courageous act when only Juan Ramon Jimenez of his own older generation of Spanish poets and thinkers joined him, when Machado's own brother, Manuel, supported the Nationalists, led by Franco. And he not only declared himself once, he did so repeatedly. He wrote and published poems about the war, about Garcia Lorca's murder, about Madrid standing against the fascist onslaught. He participated in anti-fascist writers' congresses. He contriubted to Republican magazines. He spoke on the radio. He signed petitions and declarations. He published a book titled La guerra, in 1937, in the middle of the war. And he did all this while moving, while mourning the loss of his health, and his home, his books, his friends; from Madrid to Valencia in late November 1936, to Barcelona in 1938, across the border to France in early 1939.

He declared himself openly, who he was and what he believed. He said he was not a Marxist but that he believed socialism was the great hope of humanity of that age; he was a man committed to the good and the good as he saw it was completely identified with the Republic, led by their freely elected

Socialist leaders. Evil was incarnate in the attacking fascists and those Spanish "senoritos" who supported them. His pen was turned to new concerns by those currents of his life and he wrote with passion and conviction, though always connected to those vast reservoirs of his solitude.

Now that these long censored writings are finally appearing in Spain it is time that our own more subtle and powerful censorship give way — that which proclaiming the Word of literary judgement declares them not worth printing. We are not served, in poetry or in life, by such narrow accounting of poetic value.

Machado was a poet through whom life moved and was revealed in remarkable writings. We want to see the whole of them though they may persuade us of the importance of resistance to evil as well as of the lush richness of solitude, of fountains and trees and mourning doves.

LETTER TO DAVID VIGODSKY

My Dear and Distant Friend,

Your kind letter of January 25 (1937) reached me after some delay and I would have answered by return mail if my habitual ailments hadn't been complicated by a disease of the eyes which has prevented my writing for several days.

In effect, I am old and sick, although you in your goodness don't want to believe it: old, because I am over sixty, which are many years for a Spaniard; sick because my organism's most important inner workings have all agreed to not fully comply with their mission. I think, nevertheless, that there is something in me which seems to imply health and youthful spirit—if that too isn't a sign of senility, regressing to the happy belief in the duality of matter.

But anyway my dear Vigodsky, I am with you at the side of young and healthy Spain, with all my heart at the side of the people and with all my heart against the black forces—and they are so black!—to which you allude in your letter.

The best of Spain is the people. Because of this the heroic and self sacrificing defense of Madrid which has astonished the world, has stirred me, but it doesn't surprise me. It has always been the same. In difficult moments, the senoritos—our little barons—invoke the fatherland and then sell it out; the people never speak about it but they buy it with their blood and they save it. In Spain there is no way to be well born without loving the people. Demophilia among us is a profoundly elemental debt of gratitude.

I have seen with profound satisfaction the intense current of sympathy towards Russia that has surged up in Spain. This current is, perhaps, much deeper than many believe. Because it can't be totally explained by the heroic circumstances in which it was produced, as though coinciding with Karl Marx and the communist experience, which is the great fact of the world today. No. From beneath and above and through Marxism, Spain loves Russia, feels drawn to the Russian soul. I said it more than fifteen years ago at a fiesta we celebrated in Segovia to collect funds to send to the Russian children. "Russia and Spain will meet one day as two deeply christian people, when the two shake off the yoke of the church that separates us."

Some months ago, reading THE ADOLESCENT by Dostoevsky—your great Dostoevsky—I came across a few pages, prophetic in my opinion, that affirmed the idea I had always had of the Russian soul. A character in this novel, Versilov, talking with his son—I recall this and cite it from memory because my books have remained in Madrid—says that a day will come when men will live without God. And when that great source of energy that has warmed and fortified their souls is exhausted men will feel themselves orphaned and alone. But, he adds—and this, in my judgement, is specifically Russian—that he has never been able to imagine men as depraved beings or as ingrates. Then men will embrace each other more intimately and lovingly than ever, they will shake hands with unusual emotion understanding that, from that day on, they will, each one, be for the other. The idea and feeling of immortality will be made up for by the feeling of love. It is so clearly seen that Dostoevsky is a soul so impregnated with christianity that not even in the days of the greatest destitution and blackest aetheism could he conceive of the absence of a specifically christian sentiment. And Versilov says it expressly at the end of his discourse, in these or similar words: Among the lonely and orphaned I see Christ stretching out his arms and shouting to them: "How could you have forgotten me?"

As the teacher of christianity, the Russian soul, which has learned how to capture the specifically christian, the fraternal feeling of love emancipated from the bonds of blood, will find a profound echo in the Spanish soul; not in that of Calderon (de la Barca), ecclesiastical and baroque, but in that of Cervantes, our generous and noble don Quixote who is, in my judgement, truly of the people, not at all catholic, in the sectarian sense of the word, but of the human and universally christian.

One of the greatest goods I hope for from the popular triumph is our greater closeness with Russia, the greater diffusion of its language and its great literature, still little and badly known amongst us through that, nevertheless, has left a very deep imprint in Spain.

With all my heart I thank you as a Spaniard for the work to which you now dedicate yourself as a lover of Spain. I have heard the best words about it through our friend Rafael Alberti.

Now you tell me of your translation of "The Prodigious Magician" the magnificent drama of Calderon de la Barca. The theatre of Calderon is, in my judgement, the great cathedral in the jesuit style of our baroque literature. Your translation to the Russian language will fill all lovers of our literature with pride and satisfaction.

About the tragedy of Unamuno, which is Spain's tragedy, I published some remarks in the House of Culture's first Journal. I recopy it now, slightly retouched to correct an important error in the text. It goes this way: "At the death of don Miguel de Unamuno, Juan Mairena would have said: [1] Of all the great thinkers who have made death the essential theme of their meditations, it was Unamuno who least spoke of resigning oneself to it. Such was the anti-senequist note—original and very Spanish nevertheless—of this tireless poet of Spanish anguish (angustia). Because Unamuno was anything but a stoic, that is to say, anything but a teacher of resignation to the fate of dying many denied this master of philosophy, which he was to the highest degree. Criticism, nevertheless, ought to indicate that coincident with Unamuno's last years, an entire existentialist metaphysic flowered in Europe, profoundly human, which held Unamuno not only among its adepts but also—we say this frankly—among its precursors. We will talk at length about this some other day. Today we want to make note of Unamuno's sudden death, like he who dies in a war. Against whom? Perhaps against himself, but also, though many won't believe it, against those men who have sold out Spain and have betrayed its people. Against the people itself? I have never believed it nor will I ever.

The death of Garcia Lorca has greatly saddened me. Federico was one of the two great young Andalusian poets. The other is Rafael Alberti. Both, in my judgement, complement each other as expressions of two aspects of the Andalusian homeland: the oriental (eastern) and the Atlantic. Lorca, more rooted in folklore and in the countryside was genuinely and essentially from Granada. Alberti, son of a finis terrie, the flat plains of Cadiz where the landscape disappears, the human profile is outlined against a backdrop of sea or salt marshes, is a more universal poet, but no less is, in his way, an Andalusian. A stupid crime has put out Federico's voice forever. Rafael visits the fighting fronts and, accompanied by his brave wife, Maria Teresa Leon, exposes himself to the gravest risks.

Rereading the verses I dedicated to Garcia Lorca, something I rarely do, I find the barely aesthetically elaborated expression of a direct thought, which furthermore, influenced by the unconsciousness, sine qua non of all poetry, is a sentiment of bitter complaint and is, implicitly an accusation against Granada. Granada is, I believe, one of the most beautiful cities on the world and is the cradle of many illustrious Spaniards; it is also one of the dullest cities in Spain, the most stupefied by its isolation and by the influence of its degraded and idle aristocracy, of its irredeemably provincial bourgeoisie. Could Granada have defended its poet? I believe so. It would have been easy to prove to the Fascist executioners that Lorca was politically innocuous, and that the people Federico loves and whose songs he collected were not precisely those who sing the International.

In Liberated Madrid or in Free Leningrad, I would also hold it the greatest pleasure to shake your hand. For the present I am in Valencia (Rocafort) alongside the hundred times legitimate government of the glorious Spanish Republic, with no other aspiration than to not close my eyes before seeing the definitive triumph of the people's cause, which is—as you say so well—the common cause of all progressive humanity.

Finally, dear Vigodsky, I don't want to divert your attention anymore. Affection to your son, the young baptizer of his canaries with the names of Spanish rivers. Tell him that his charming homage to the memory of the well loved poet has moved me greatly.

I am at your orders, your good friend

Antonio Machado

P.S. I send you these drawings by my brother Jose so you can see some authentic graphic views of Our Spain.

Valencia, April 1937

1   Juan de Mairena is one of several literary figures invented by Machado as a "double" to speak philosophically and literarily rather than poetically.

Translated by Will Kirkland

ADDRESS TO THE UNIFIED SOCIALIST YOUTH

Perhaps the best counsel I can give a young person is that he truly be so. I know this advice will seem superfluous to many. In my judgement, it isn't. Because it can always be used to counter the opposite counsel which is implicit in a perverse education: try to be old as soon as possible.

The purity of childhood is watched over; it is defended, above all, from the dangers of an early puberty. Very few watch over the purity of youth; very few are disturbed by the danger, no less grave, of premature old age. We know now and perhaps have always believed, that infancy does not become confused by itself; we have acquired a repect for the child which, in truth, is laudable, if it doesn't come to border on idolatry. On the other hand, people continue to believe that all the turbulance we observe in the young comes from youthful sources. I have always thought the opposite. Because of that I have always said to the young: go on with your youth. Not that it should go beyond its natural limits in time, but that within it, you should live it fully. And above all, go on with your youthful tasks: they are absolutely not transferable. No one will do them if you don't.

One of Spain's greatest sins, perhaps the greatest, that today we are perhaps purging in this tragedy of our fatherland, is that which we might call, "the greatest sin of old adolescents." I know them well, dear friends. Forgive me this small boast. In my, by now long life, I have seen various groups and graduating classes of young people march by, perverted by age: churchrats, putrid flowers, repugnant worms from filthy sewers. I know them well. And it is these same youths who today, now matured, or better, now rotted, that rise up at the rearguard of their mercenary armies as the standards of reaction; those same who decided, coldly and cowardly, to sell out their country and betray the future of its people. It is these same people also who today, although it doesn't seem so, would like to corrupt you, to sow confusion in your ranks. They are enemies of your discipline, whatever ideals they claim to profess.

Discipline! There is a word which you, young and unified socialist youth don't need, fortunately, but of which I remind you here. You know that discipline, necessary for achievement

51

in all human enterprises, is indispensable in war time. You, as youth, know much more discipline than we, the old, could have taught you. Contrary to what is believed, or is pretended to be believed, discipline is an essentially youthful virtue which very seldom reaches into old age. Only that age which is generous to all the possibilities of the future can, with pleasure, sacrifice all small minded individuality to the iron collective norms imposed by ideals. Only the truly young know how to obey their captains without humiliation; to be solicitous, without a shadow of adulation, of the prestige of the men who at the moments of danger handle the tillers of our ships; it is only they who know that in time of war and storm the captains and pilots, when they are in their places, are sacred.

I have no fear of youthful indiscipline because I have never believed there was such. I fear a great deal; I have always feared a great deal, from the meek indiscipline of old age, that anarchic old age, in the perjorative sense of these words, (a gray haired old man engaged in heroic actions knows how to guard the pure flame of his youth as a treasure, and a true anarchist can be a saint), with its spirit which is uncontrollable and rebellious to all ideas, always miserly with material goods, covetous of command in order to impose servitude, in other words, that which obeys the most grossly individual; the humors, the appetites of his brokendown body, his most disturbed spite, his most ephemeral lusts. I have always feared this, which is age itself.

If you observe the brief history of our Republic, which was magnificently innaugurated with all the indications of youth, under control of men who governed and legislated, attentive to the future of their people, you will see that it is a profoundly old man, the decrepit soul of a soft and broken down whore, Lerroux by name, who is in charge of bringing it down, of mounting over it—our noble Republic!—all the rubbish of a ruined and rancid politics, all the muck of an inexhaustable Spanish villany. And he calls this, extending the base of the Republic.

I salute you then, young unified socialists, with the respect I have not always been able to feel for the old, of my own era, because many of them are unmaking Spain, and you intend to re-make it. From a theoretical point of view I am not a Marxist.

I never have been and it is very possible I never will be. My thoughts haven't followed the trail that has descended from Hegel to Karl Marx. Perhaps because I am too romantic, from the influence of too idealistic an education, I lack an affinity for the central idea of Marxism; I resist believing that the economic factor, whose enormous importance I am not unfamiliar with, is the most essential factor of human life and the great motor of history. Nevertheless, I see clearly that Socialism, in as much as it implies a way of human coexistence, based on work, on the equality of means granted to all for its realization, and on the abolition of the privileges of class, is an unavoidable step on the road to justice; I see clearly that this is the great human experience of our time to which everyone ought to contribute in some way. It coincides fully with your youth and is a magnificent labor, don't ever doubt it. So it is, that not only as true youth but also as socialists I salute you with all my warmth.

And in as much as you have learned to unify yourselves, which is much more than just to have meetings, or to come together to make noise, count on all my sympathy and my most sincere admiration.

May 1, 1937

Translated by Will Kirkland

THE POET AND THE PEOPLE

(On the defense and diffusion of culture. An ad
given in Valencia in the closing session of the
International Congress of Writers, August, 1937)

When someone asked me, many years ago: "Do you think a poet ought to write for the people or stay locked up in an ivory tower—it was the topic in fashion in those days—dedicated to an aristocratic art, in realms of culture accessible only to a select minority?" I answered with these words, which to many seemed a little evasive or ingenuous: "To write for the people— as my teacher said—what more could I want? Desirous of writing for the people I learned from him as much as I could, much less it is clear, than he knows. To write for the people is, minimally, to write for the man of our race, of our land, of our speech; three things with inexhaustible content, which we will never fully know. But it is much more, because to write for the people obliges us to go beyond the frontiers of our homeland and to write for men of other races also, of other lands and other tongues. To write for the people is to be called Cervantes in Spain, Shakespeare in England, Tolstoy in Russia. It is the miracle of the geniuses of the word. Perhaps some of them accomplished it without being aware of it, without even having desired it. But the day will come when it will be the most conscious and supreme aspiration of the poet. As far as this concerns me, a mere apprentice in poetic wisdom, I don't believe I have gone beyond being a folklorist, an apprentice in my own way, to popular wisdom."

My reply was that of a Spaniard, conscious of his Hispanitude, who knows, who must know, that in Spain almost everything that is great is a work by the people or for the people; that in Spain the truly aristocratic is, in a certain way, of the people. In the early months of the war that soaks Spain in blood, when the fight hadn't yet lost its aspect of being a purely civil war, I wrote these words with the intention of verifying my democratic faith, my belief in the superiority of the people over the privileged classes.

54

THE MILICIANOS OF 1936

> After putting his life as his law
> so many times on the table...

I

Why do I always remember this phrase of don Jorge Manrique[1] when I see, leafing through newspapers and magazines, the pictures of our <u>milicianos?</u> Perhaps it is because these men, not exactly soldiers but a people in arms, have in their faces the grave visage, the concentrated expression of the invisible, of those who, as the poet says, "put on the table, their lives as their law," who play this singular money—if they lose there is no other—for a deeply felt cause. The truth is that all these <u>milicianos</u> seem to be captains, so present is the noble senorio (majesty) of their faces..

II

When a great city—like Madrid in these days—lives through a tragic experience, its physiognomy changes, and we notice a strange phenomenon in it, compensating for so many hardships: the sudden disappearance of the senorito. And it is not, as some think, that the senorito flees or hides, but that he disappears—literally—, he is erased; the human tragedy erases him; the man erases him. The truth is, as Juan de Mairena[2] said, there aren't any senoritos, but only 'senoritismo,' one form among many of degraded manhood, a peculiar style of not being a man, which can be observed at times in individuals of all social classes, and has nothing to do with starched collars, neckties or the shine of the boots.

III

Among us, Spaniards, not at all senoritos by nature, senoritismo is an epidermical disease whose origin can be found perhaps, in our jesuitical education, so profoundly anti-christian and—we say this with pride—absolutely anti-Spanish. Because senoritismo implicitly carries with it an erroneous and servile judgement which puts those no more than superficial social facts—signs of class, habits and clothing—before those values correctly understood, which are religious and human. Senoritismo ignores, is pleased to ignore—jesuitically—the insuperable dignity of man. The people on the other hand know it and affirm it; in it the ethic of the people has its most solid foundation. "No man is better than another," runs an adage from Castile. A perfect expression of modesty and pride! Yes, "No man is better than another," because it is given to no one to take advantage for himself over everyone, since over everyone there are those who win in circumstances of time and place. "No man is better than another," because—and this is the deepest meaning of the phrase—however much a man is worth he will never have more value than that of being a man. So speaks Castile, a people of senores, which has never thought much of senoritos.

IV

When in the ancient poem, el Cid,[3] el senor, with a manliness acclaimed by his own enemies, makes ready to break the siege the Moors had put around Valencia, he calls to his wife, dona Jimena, and to his daughters, Elvira and Sol, so they can see "how bread is earned." This is the divine modesty with which Rodrigo (el Cid) speaks of his own deeds. It is this same man, however, who suffers banishment for having stood up before the King, Alphonso, and demanded of him, man to man, to swear on the gospels, that he does not owe his crown to fratracide.[4] And in that immortal epic, alongside the Cid, that great master of himself, appear the two Infantes de Carrion,[5] cowardly, vengeful and vain, those felonious senoritos, with the definitive stamp of a rigidifying aristocracy. Someone has suggested, with sure insight, that the poem of the Cid is of the struggle between a rising democracy and a declining aristocracy. I would say, better, between Castilian manliness and Leonese senoritismo of that era.

V

There will be no lack of those who think that the shadows of the Cid's sons-in-law[6] today accompany the fascist armies and counsel them to such deeds as that of "Robledo de Corpes."[7] I myself won't claim as much, as I don't like to denigrate the adversary. But I believe with all my soul that Rodrigo's shadow accompanies our own heroic <u>milicianos</u> and that in God's wisdom, today, as took place then on the banks of the Tagus, the better men will win again. Or it would have to be an insult to the same divinity.

Madrid, August, 1936

1 *Spanish poet, 1440-1479.*

2 *One of Machado's invented characters through whom he spoke in matters of philosophy.*

3 *El Cid, the famous knightly guerillero of 11th century Spain, Rodrigo Diaz de Bivar, immortalized in many songs and legends, the best known of which is El Poema del Mio Cid.*

4 *El Cid originally supported Alphonso's brother, Sancho, in the struggle for the divided kingdoms of Spain bequeathed by their father Ferdinand. Sancho won but was latter killed in a battle, leaving the throne empty, to which Alphonso came — leading to the Cid's demand of him.*

5 *The Infantes de Carrion were wealthy aristocrats from Leon. When Rodrigo (El Cid), decidedly not an aristocrat, had regained the King's favor with a series of awesome battles against the Moors and had become rich from all the booty, the Infantes asked for and received Rodrigo's daughters in marriage. Having proved themselves cowards by hiding from an unleashed lion while others surrounded Rodrigo to shield him, they showed their villany by taking their wives into the wilds, stripping them and beating them and leaving them for dead.*

6 *The Infantes de Carrion, above.*

7 *A small town in the province of Guadalajara; the event referred to I haven't discovered yet.*

Among Spaniards, the essentially human is found in its greatest purity and sharpest relief in the soul of the people. I don't know if the same can be said of other countries; my knowledge of folklore hasn't gone beyond the frontiers of my homeland. But I dare to affirm that in Spain the aristocratic prejudice that of writing exclusively for the best, can be accepted and even converted into the literary norm, only with this admonition: the Spanish aristocracy is of the people; writing for the people is to write for the best. If we were, sanctimoniously, to wish not to exclude the so called upper classes from the pleasures of popular literature, we would have to lower the human level and the aesthetic levels of the works that the people have made their own, and mix frivolities and pedantries into them. In a more or less conscious way our classics have often done this. Everything superfluous in <u>El Quijote</u> comes not from concessions made to

57

popular taste, or as it was said then, to the stupidity of the vulgar, but on the contrary, from those made to the aesthetic perversion of the court. Someone has said, in a puffed up phrase, unacceptable ad pedem litterae, but with a deep sense of the truth: in our literature almost everything that isn't folklore is pedantry.

But leaving to one side the Spanish aspect, or better said—the Spanishish aspect—of the question that is contained, in my judgement, in this clear dilemma: either we write without forgetting the people or we write only foolishness. Returning to the universal aspect of the problem, which is the diffusion and defense of culture, I'm going to read you the words of Juan de Mairena, an apocryphal or hypothetical professor who planned a Popular School of Higher Wisdom for our homeland.

* * *

Culture, seen from afar, by those who never contribute to its creation, may seem to be a hoard of cash or merchandise, which when divided among many, among the most, would not be sufficient to enrich anyone. Diffusion of culture would be for those who think this—if this is to think—a waste or a squandering of the culture, to be truly lamented. That is so logical!... But it is strange that it is the anti-marxists, who fight against the materialist interpretation of history, who expound such a materialist conception of cultural diffusion.

In effect, culture seen from afar, as though we were speaking from ignorance or, again, from pedantry, might seem to be a treasure whose possession and custody are the privilege of a few; and the yearning for culture which people feel, and its increase in the people, to which we would like to contribute, appear as threats against a sacred deposit. But we who see culture from within, I mean to say—from man himself—think neither of a hoard, nor of a treasure, nor of a deposit of culture, as though they were funds or times that could be piled up on one side or the other and haphazardly passed out, much less be sacked by the mobs.

For us, to defend and diffuse culture is one and the same thing: to augment the human treasure of vigilant consciousness in the world. How? By waking up those who sleep. As long as the numbers of those wakened is greater... For me—as Juan de Mairena used to say—there could only be one reason of note which would prevent a great diffusion of culture, or movement of culture which is now concentrated in a narrow circle of the elite, or privileged, to other, wider fields; that would be if we were to verify that Carnot's principle also governs that class of energy, the spiritual, which wakes the sleeping. In this case we would have to proceed with the utmost caution because an excessive diffusion of culture would imply, when the accounts were tallied, a degradation of the same, such that it would be practically useless. But, in my judgement, nothing has been verified about the applicability of Carnot to spiritual energy. We might just as well, though not at all seriously, propose the contrary thesis which, in accordance with the most obvious evidence, would affirm the constant reversibility of that spiritual energy which produces culture.

* * *

For us culture neither comes from an energy that deteriorates on propagation, nor is it wealth that diminishes on being distributed; its defense will come about as the result of a generous activity which implicitly carries within it, the two deepest paradoxes of ethics: only that which is held onto is lost; only that which is given away is gained.

Teach this to those who don't know it. Wake the sleeping. Call at the doors of all hearts, of all consciousnesses. And, because it is not man who is created for culture but culture which is created for man, for all men and for each man—but in no way a huge burden to be carried aloft by all men, it being of such a nature that its weight can only be carried if distributed among all—if tomorrow a gale of cynicism, of elemental humanity, shakes the tree of culture and carries away more than just its dry leaves, don't be afraid. Trees that are too heavy have to lose some of their branches in favor of the fruit. Lacking a knowledgeable and careful pruning, a hurricane might do as well.

* * *

When Juan de Mairena was asked if the poet, and in general the writer, ought to write for the masses, he answered: Be careful friends. There is a man of the people who is, in Spain at least, an elemental and fundamental man and who is nearer to us than some universal and eternal man. The mass man doesn't exist: the human masses are inventions of the bourgeoisie, a degradation of the multitudes of men, based on a depreciation of man, which wants to reduce him to that which he has in common with the objects of the physical world: volume. Mistrust the cliche, "the human masses." Many well intentioned people, our best friends, use it today without realizing that it comes from the enemy camp: that of the bourgeois capitalist who exploits man and who must degrade him; there is in it something also of the Church, an organ of power, which more than once has proclaimed itself the supreme institution for the salvation of the masses. Be careful; no one saves the masses; on the other hand it is always possible to fire a volley on their behalf. Watch out!

Many of the most difficult to solve problems raised by the poetry of the future—the continuation of an enduring art in new circumstances of time and place—and the failure of some well intentioned tentative solutions, comes in part from this: to write for the masses is to write for no one, and less than anything, for man himself, for those millions of human consciences, scattered all over the world and who fight, as in Spain, so heroically and boldly to destroy all the obstacles put in the way of the integrity of their manhood, to take control of the means that will permit them to become one with that manhood. If you direct yourselves to the masses, the man, the individual man who listens to you won't feel himself related to and will necessarily turn his back on you.

This is the maliciousness carried by the falsity implicit in enemies of all cultural senoritismo, will never use, from a respect and a love for the people which our adversaries will never feel.

Valencia, August, 1937

Translated by Will Kirkland

A HOMAGE TO MACHADO IN 1966

A day set aside to honor Antonio Machado, the great Spanish poet who died in exile in southern France in 1939, had been announced for the 20th of February, 1966. The homage, notice of which was given all government bureaus concerned, was to consist of the unveiling of a monument to Machado—a bronze head made by the sculptor Pablo Serrono. The bust would be unveiled in the town of Baeza (Jaen) where Machado had taught French for several years in the local school; the monument was to be placed at a spot outside of town, a particularly lovely spot often visited by Machado in his walks. The homage was announced under the title "Walks With Antonia Machado."

The committee that organized it was heterogeneous, including the judge in Baeza as well as many writers and artists living in Madrid. The Spanish Press gave considerable publicity to the plans for the homage. Several days before it, the weekly Triunfo in Madrid published a full page photograph of the bronze bust, now finished, as illustration to an article written by Moreno Galva; at the same time a number of papers published declarations of support for the homage, plus various other testimonies of public sympathy for the project.

The day before the homage, a brief note appeared in several papers, its origin unknown, declaring that the homage had been cancelled. By that time, most of the people who had intended to be there were already from various parts of Spain— from Alicante, Seville, Cordoba, Valencia, Barcelona, Bilbao, Madrid,...

The "Guardia Civil," armed with submachine guns, waited for the cars on all the roads around Baeza, several kilometers from the city limits. They stopped all buses, but let private cars go through, at least in the beginning, though not without noting down the license numbers. Many people walked into town from that spot later when private cars were halted.

Under these circumstances some 2,500 people arrived in Baeza on the 20th, not counting another large group who did not succeed in breaking through the police line. The daily paper Jaen declared that: "Today Baeza will render a homage to Machado." The crowd of people moved out of town toward the area of the monument. The line was long and silent, but the mood was a mood of affection and comaraderie among the admirers of the poet. Shortly before the line arrived at the spot, some "Armed Police" (popularly called the Greys because of their uniform) appeared and blocked the road. Several participants walked forward to ask for an explanation, which the police refused. A lieutenant arrived, and soon police reinforcements. There was great tension. The police lieutenant said flatly that the gathering was cancelled, and that they had orders to keep the people away from the place in question. He said he did not know the reasons why. He was asked to make known to some authority—the Mayor of the city or the Govenor of the province—the unanimous desire of those present that some explanation be given them for what was taking place. The lieutenant refused this and threatened to charge on the group. Those present pressed together in lines and made known their decision to wait there for the arrival of someone in power who would give them a good explanation. The effort these people had gone through to get there, many from places far away, should not be made to end in a simple return home under the arbitrary order of some member of the state police or an official of the constabulary.

The lieutenant took a step backward and blew a whistle. The police drew up in lines and took out their clubs. The lieutenant read a paragraph referring to "violations of the laws of Public Order" and announced that at the third blow of the whistle, the police "would charge" against persons present. Those present linked arms tightly, prepared to hold to their decision to wait for a decent explanation of the cancellation.

The charge began. The "Greys" held back a moment. The officer drew his pistol and shouted, "Charge! Charge!" A policeman also from the Political-Social Brigade waved his pistol as if he were fencing, furious, absolutely out of his mind. "Charge! Charge!."

From then on it was brutality and violence. The crowd cried: "Murderer! Murderer!" Many fell down under the blows. Groans, cries, young people sobbed with fear. The Greys pursued savagely the few people who ran in the first moments, and continued to beat those who remained standing, both those facing the police and those trying to help others on the ground.

The large mass of people, after returning two kilometers

back to town, filed into the Main Plaza of Baeza in a mood of rage, exasperation and fear. Some took shelter in bars or cafes from which the police expelled them by force back to the street where they were met with more violence; blows, insults and various indignities. Many arrests took place and the tracking began —the pursuit of people into every nook of town: new arrests and high-handedness.

The town watched this sight astonished. "Get to your cars!" the Greys shouted, pushing heavily against anyone and everyone. The deputies from the Political-Social Brigade assisted them on all sides. Those who had no cars to leave town with were thwacked, chased, hunted into any shelter they could take. A long parade of cars fled by all the highways leading out, and those who arrived Ubeda (a nearby town) could see the officers in the Guardia Civil barracks waiting for the order to go to Baeza.

This is what happened to the homage for Antonio Machado in Baeza the 20th of February, 1966.

Twenty-seven people were arrested, among them Jose Monero Galvan (author of the article mentioned above); Pedro Caba (doctor); Eduardo Urculo (painter); Manuel Aguilar (publisher); Roberto Puig (architect); Cortijo (painter); Pipolles (painter); Alfredo Florez (lawyer); J.A. Ramos Herranz (engineer); Pedro Dicenta (teacher); Carlos Alvarez (poet), etc.

Of the twenty arrested, sixteen were released just before dawn. Eleven remained in jail, and were taken to Jaen and released there the next day after they had paid fines varying according to the case from 5,000 pesatos to 10,000, 15,000 and 25,000 pasetas.

The report of an eye-witness

Translated from the Spanish by
Robert Bly

Dennis Maloney

MACHADO IN TRANSLATION

I Never Wanted Fame—translated by Robert Bly: Ally Press, PO Box 30340 St. Paul, Minn. 55175 ($2.50)

Canciones—translated by Robert Bly: Toothpaste Press, PO Box 546, 626 E. Main St., West Branch, Ia. 52358 ($4.00)

Times Alone—translated by Robert Bly: Greywolf Press, PO Box 142, Port Townsend, WA 98363 ($5.00)

Antonio Machado—Selected Poems—translated by Alan S. Trueblood: Harvard University Press, 79 Garden St., Cambridge, Ma. 02138 ($25.00)

The Dream Below The Sun, Selected Poems of Antonio Machado—translated by Willis Barnstone: Crossing Press, Trumansburg, NY 14886 ($7.95)

It is characteristic, perhaps, that all three of Machado's main translators have stayed with his work for many years. Willis Barnstone began translating Machado in college and his Eighty Poems of Machado, published in 1959 and long out of print, was for years the only Machado work available in English. Shortly after the idea of this issue was first conceived in 1980, Crossing Press republished an expanded and revised edition of Barnstone's book under the title, The Dream Below The Sun. The new edition contains a healthy and representative selection of Machado's poems as well as wonderful reminiscence of Machado by fellow poet, Juan Ramon Jimenez. The translations are capable and the volume serves as a good introduction to the poems.

Robert Bly has been translating Machado for over twenty five years and Machado's work was a prime influence on Bly's own first book, Silence in the Snowy Fields. Until Bly's larger selection arrives later this year what we have are three handsome, finely printed letterpress chapbooks of ten to twelve poems each. My favorite among the three is I Never Wanted Fame which contains ten short poems from Machado's proverbs and songs including one of the first Machado poems I read and have carried with me over ten years:

> Mankind owns four things
> that are no good at sea:
> rudder, anchor, oars
> and the fear of going down.

Canciones is also made up of ten tiny poems, from another collection of the songs, while Times Alone, contains twelve poems from Machado's first book, Soledades. I find Robert Bly's translations the most sucessful of the three translators here, at carrying over the spirit of the original; creating what becomes a fine poem in contemporary American language.

Alan S. Trueblood, in his volume, presents us with a useful introduction to Machado's life and poetry. Through a lengthy introduction and extensive annotated notes on the poems he provides a fine scholarly presentation for the serious student of Machado's work who desires further background on the poet and his work. His translations are adequate but often suffer from a too literal rendering into English.

With these volumes, recognition of Machado as one of the great poets of this century seems assured in an America where his work was virtually unknown until recently.

CONTRIBUTOR NOTES

Robert Bly is one of our most accomplished translators and has translated from several languages. His recent books of translations include the Selected Poems of Rainer Marie Rilke and Times Alone, a chapbook of poems by Antonio Machado. His selected poems of Machado will appear later this year from Wesleyan Press. The most recent book of his own poetry is The Man In The Black Coat Turns. Will Kirkland lives in San Francisco and teaches English as a second language while he writes and translates, from the Castillian, Catalan and Basque. His work has appeared in many periodicals including American Poetry Review and the New Directions Anthology #45. His translation of Federico Garcia Lorca, The Cricket Sings: Songs and Poems for Children, was published by New Directions in 1980. Carmen Scholis and William Witherup translated I Go Dreaming Roads, a collection of Machado's poems, long out of print, from which several poems here were drawn. William Witherup's books include Bixby Creek Poems and Four From Kentucky.

PRESS NEWS

The next issue of White Pine Journal due out in March, 1983 will be a double issue devoted to the work of Joel Oppenheimer. It will feature transcripts edited from several talks given by Oppenheimer in Buffalo in which he speaks on his poetics, The Women Poems, Black Mountain and other topics. The issue will also contain a selection of his poems, both old and new, a checklist of his work and an introductory essay by David Landrey, who guest edits this issue—$6.00

Recent titles from the press include: The View From Cold Mountain, poems of zen poets Han-shan and Shih-te translated by Tobias, Seaton and Stanford—$4.00 A Concoctionist Cookbook by Judy Trupin, a vegetarian sugar-free cookbook—$4.50. Stem a book of poems by David Giannini—$3.00

Subscriptions to the Journal are $12.00 for four issues. Send for a full catalog of press titles. Add $.75 postage on all book orders.

White Pine Press, 73 Putnam St., Buffalo, NY 14213